TRAMWAY ART

TRAMWAY ART

The distinctive poster art of the
London County Council tramways
surveyed by Jonathan Riddell

Capital Transport

FOREWORD

Nicolette Tomkinson
Director, Christie's Vintage Poster Department

This journey through the LCC tramways posters leaves you with an overwhelming desire to visit the array of open spaces and the thought of how fantastic it is that Londoners have such a variety of attractions from fabulous parks, common land, to theatreland and museums.

Although the tram was considered a more working class mode of transport, the 1929 'Pullman Tramcar' poster by René Blair shows elegantly dressed ladies engaged in conversation after a day's shopping relaxing on upholstered seats. Next to them sits a man leisurely studying the daily news clearly very comfortable in the clean, light and airy carriage. The poster successfully conveys the message that to travel by tram was to travel 'the modern way'. Similarly in Herbert Kerr Rooke's 1926 poster the message 'travel by tram' was promoted 'For Speedy Travel and Sheltered Comfort'.

LCC tramway poster campaigns were also focused on encouraging people to travel off-peak to ease congestion during busy times. This was a theme that was also explored by the London Underground publicity posters. Interestingly the Underground posters of the same period were often designed by established commercial artists and big names in the art world. By contrast the LCC tramway images are no less striking and yet were designed by students and indeed may have been their first commercial undertaking.

The posters also offer us a glimpse into how the Londoners of the 1920s spent their leisure time. The posters promote the attractions of strolling through Battersea and Greenwich parks, boating in Hyde Park and encourage travel further afield to experience the changing seasons at Kew Gardens. In north London, Hampstead Heath and Kenwood were heavily promoted. Oliver Burridge's 1924 poster for Highgate is particularly successful in conveying the attractions of the village feel of Highgate in the centre of London.

The Zoo is an area where the tramway posters excel. Frank Marsden Lea's portrayal of the striking flamingoes (1932), Van Jones's colourful and friendly parrots (1927), Edmunds's swinging monkeys (1928) and Tony Castle's dramatic South American toucans (1929) would have been a welcome splash of colour through London's streets.

Travelling by tram was the most economical means of travelling around London and was a good option for exploring London's heritage. Many of the posters promote a sightseeing tour of London by tram taking in the sights of Tower Bridge, Westminster Abbey and St Paul's cathedral – sightseeing tours the Underground could never compete with.

In the auction world the LCC tramway images are relatively unknown. Aside from a private collection we were honoured to handle here at Christie's in sales between 2004–2006 they very rarely appear on the market. The posters were produced in two standard sizes the smallest of which now makes them the perfect size to fit into today's interiors, so when they do come up for sale they are now very sought after.

Buyers will be looking for a striking image, but will overwhelming collect by location be it Hampstead Heath, Putney, Wimbledon or St James's Park. Most of the images in this book are previously unpublished and provide a visual treat for anyone interested in London, graphic design and poster art.

First published 2010

ISBN 978-1-85414-334-1

Published by Capital Transport Publishing
www.capitaltransport.com

Printed by 1010 Printing International in China

Text © Jonathan Riddell 2010

Acknowledgements

The staff of the London Metropolitan Archives have been very helpful in the compilation of this book. Nicolette Tomkinson at Christies also helped with the supply of images. The posters on pages 13 top centre and top right, 24, 25, 31, 44, 60 and 115 are from the London Transport Museum collection. The map cover on page 96 was supplied by Dave Jones of the LCC Tramways Trust.

CONTENTS

INTRODUCTION

Before the formation of the London Passenger Transport Board in 1933, the London County Council Tramways (LCCT) was one of several organisations providing public transport across London. Although the LCC was the largest operator of tramways in the capital, the Underground Group dominated London's transport scene, controlling most of London's buses, Underground railways and also three tramway companies, namely the Metropolitan Electric Tramways, South Metropolitan Electric Tramways and London United Tramways. There was very little competition from the Underground's trams since the two networks served different areas of London with only limited joint running. However, there was competition from the Underground's railways and buses. As early as the 1920s the council was aware that the real competition with the LCC's trams was with the Underground's buses, which even in LCCT days was beginning to foretell the eventual demise of London's tramway network.

In response to this competition, and aware of the high standard of the Underground's publicity, the council eventually decided to improve the tramways' publicity. In 1922, when the LCCT began to issue its first pictorial posters, the Underground Group – London's biggest and best known transport operator – was already well known for the design of its stations and posters. Since 1908 the Underground under Frank Pick had commissioned posters directly from many of the leading artists of the day and had established its predominance as a patron of poster art in Britain. The LCCT could not fail to see the success of the Underground's bright and colourful posters, displayed as they were across London. However, it was slow to follow the example so admirably set by the Underground. It was not until 14 years later, in 1922, that at last the LCCT realised that the advertising space on its tramcars could and should be used for anything other than other companies' commercial advertising. After all an advertising site let to another company brought in immediate revenue whereas a site used to advertise its own services brought in no immediate revenue and, it could be argued, made no money for the company. However, the success of the Underground's posters could no longer be ignored and in 1922 the LCCT commissioned its first set of posters by artists to promote its services. So, on 7 February 1922 the London County Council's Highways Committee passed the following minute authorising the commissioning and display of pictorial posters in the council's tramcars.

'Tramways advertising – Display of posters
We have arranged for a series of pictorial posters to be exhibited on the Council's tramcars. Suitable sketches in black and white are to be supplied by the Council's Central School of Arts and Crafts, the total costs for a reproduction of 2000 copies of each of a series of 12 posters being £650. The posters will be designed so as to be suitable for varying times of the year. It has also been decided that alternating with the proposed pictorial posters, propaganda posters advertising the tramways system should be displayed in the cars.'

The decision to only issue black and white posters was no doubt due to concerns about the cost and effectiveness of the proposed programme. The unusual size of 28½ x 14¼in (72cm x 36cm) was so that the posters would fit the display panel at the front of the lower saloon on tramcars, where timetable and fare information had been displayed. In later years posters were issued in three sizes. The largest was 60in x 40in (152cm x 102cm), known as a 4-sheet. Some posters were also printed in the double crown size of 30in x 20in (76cm x 51cm). This size is in the same proportion as the 4 sheet size but it was the image from the smaller 28½ x 14¼in size that was used surrounded by a large blank border.

The choice of artists from the council's own art school, together with the subjects and styles, resulted in a series of highly attractive designs. It was not surprising that when the LCCT eventually decided to commission posters it commissioned them from the Central School of Arts and Crafts, which was not only one of the country's leading art schools but was run, like the tramways, by the London County Council. For many years William Lethaby, a friend of William Morris and the Central's first Principal, had spoken out at the current standard of poster design and advertising display. Lethaby was a keen believer in the importance of linking design and production, and the Central School was founded on these lines with its students taking an active role in the means of production as well as of design. The school, as befitted one run by the LCC, attracted a wide range of students from all backgrounds with a wide social mix with grants and bursaries available to those in need of them. Many of the tramways posters were designed by women, as the Central School incorporated the Royal Female School of Art in 1908 and the School had a very egalitarian policy. In the 1920s the commercial artistic world presented one of the few opportunities for women looking for professional work. Unfortunately the council's minutes only record the decisions made and shed no light as to who initiated the idea for the posters; it may originally have come from the school. Fred V Burridge, who was the school's principal at the time, must have played a leading role in persuading the tramways to commission his school's students to design a set of posters.

In 1923, encouraged by the success of their first set of 12 posters, the LCCT felt emboldened to commission further posters from the Central School, this time in colour. The first of these coloured posters advertised Caledonian Market. In February 1923 a council minute notes that tramway posters will be displayed on council premises, whilst two months later another minute records that posters will be displayed at the council's educational sites, with all costs being paid for by the tramways. In May 1924 it is recorded that further posters are being produced and in October of the same year another minute records that posters will no longer be displayed other than on LCC sites. No reason is given for this decision but it is likely that by this time the display of posters at LCC sites was so comprehensive that it was no longer felt necessary or cost effective to pay for other sites. May 1925 saw an agreement to spend up to £650 on poster boards for the council's trams and a further minute in October records that poster boards would be put up at Latchmere Road Baths and Westminster Bridge subway (but not on the stairs). Although posters continued to be issued seemingly as before, there are no further references to them in the council minutes until May 1928 when a rather puzzling minute read '*Tramway adverts – We have given instructions for the issue of a series of posters similar in character to those exhibited some years ago, directing attention to the features of the Council's tramway undertaking, with which it is desirable that the public should be familiar.*' Looking at the posters it is unclear as to why this minute was made as the poster programme appeared to have continued as before except that the posters were no longer designed by students of the council's Central School of Arts and Crafts. Perhaps it was felt that the

programme had lost direction or was in some other way in need of a boost. It was at this time that the LCCT began to issue 'Holiday' leaflets full of suggestions for day trips in London. Each suggestion was illustrated by one of the posters which had been issued during the preceding years. Whatever the reason for this concern about the tramway's publicity, there seems to have been a renewed interest in the value of the poster. During the winter of 1928-1929 the LCCT published a paper which had been read at one of its Depot Meetings at Holloway. This explained the reasons behind, and the success of, the tramways' publicity campaigns. In particular it valued the role that staff played in promoting the tramways. It must be remembered that posters were just one of many types of publicity used by the tramways and they were often used in conjunction with newspaper advertisements, leaflets and press releases to advertise the council's services. It is worth quoting at length from this paper as it so clearly sums up the council's attitude to its tramways' advertising and publicity:

'*Advertisements that inform. I mean printed lists of services, fares, timetables, an explanation of transfer facilities.*

Advertisements that attract. In this class are accounts of 1/- all-day fare excursions: illustrations and descriptions of the comfort of Pullman cars; pictures of Epping Forest and other holiday places. These things ought to induce, and do induce additional travel, especially on Saturdays, Sundays and in weekday slack hours.'

The smaller posters were designed to be displayed at the ends of the lower saloon and occasionally on the driver's platform. This view shows a poster by Lawson Wood in Car No. 1 'Bluebird', so named because of its blue livery and sleek, streamlined body. Adapted to the double crown format, they were also displayed on panels on the side next to the driver's window. *City of London, London Metropolitan Archives*

Newspaper advertisements are expensive. One insertion in the Daily Mail costs £132. Cost of space is decided by nation-wide circulation. But here in London we are interested in a paper's circulation in London, not Liverpool. So you see there are pitfalls even in Press advertising.

Pictures as a Traffic-builder
The poster offers a very big field for advertising travel facilities. It can tell its story right on the spot. It can be put just where a message is likely to have most influence. It makes possible the introduction of colour, an element to which people of all ages react very eagerly. It has been said that a street poster should be designed to be read by anyone passing at between three an hour and thirty. But that again depends on circumstances. It is true of most announcements on the outside of tramcars, not on the inside.

As for dashboards, top streamers, corners and rocker panels, these are best used for relatively short messages. Inside cars and at shelters, on the other hand, we encourage more leisurely inspection. Posters in shelters add splashes of bright colour and catch a traveller in a mood when he is very ready to be interested. We like to believe that five minutes spent in Stamford Hill Shelter waiting for a car seems like five seconds to anyone examining the posters and maps there. For larger positions we use the walls of schools, offices and works of the LCC and other public bodies. Of these positions there are 770. As a rule they stand quite alone, and on that account are very effective.

Every month the department issues a pictorial poster. Over 70 have been printed. The first one in colour epitomised Caledonian Market. Those in preparation include the Zoo and Putney. Sometimes a poster illustrates a travel feature, such as Comfort and Speed. At Christmas passengers were asked to shop early. And they did. Not once but several times.

School Children Interested
Some of the most valuable positions are in the cars themselves. Let to traders these spaces would produce hard cash. Used for advertising the Tramways they yield quite as much in increasing receipts from passengers and by building up prestige. Our posters are eagerly sought by schoolmasters and mistresses. For one picture there were 500 applications. They hang in classrooms, and are used for encouraging sightseeing and for teaching geography and history. Do you remember the poster of Victoria Embankment, the one showing a night of driving rain? A copy was bought by a Forest Hill lady. She had sons in the jungle of Burma, she said, and thought that they would be cheered up by this picture of dear old London! A magazine in the United States of America reproduced six posters with this comment, 'They make one want to travel in London's trams.' And we think so too. A Chicago store, world famous, obtains copies for exhibition in its travel bureau and also sends them round the States as part of a touring show of modern posters.

It is not enough to advertise, say, Waterlow Park outside the 'Archway' only. To do that would be to preach to the converted. Waterlow Park must be advertised here, there and everywhere. From Camden Town to Catford, at any point where there is a tramcar within half a mile or so.

Maps are displayed in business houses, hotels, public resorts and schools. This year the edition is increased to 4,200.

The posters displayed at this tram shelter at Kennington in August 1933 reflect the recent takeover of the LCC Tramways by the London Passenger Transport Board. On the top row from left to right are LCCT posters advertising Putney, Old Hampstead and St James's Park. On each of these posters a sticker can be seen bearing the words 'London Passenger Transport Board'. Beneath these are three London Transport posters advertising the Kingsway Subway and Mitcham Fair. Inside the shelter further posters and a map were displayed. The LCCT used a non-standard size for its smaller posters, so it was necessary to print some copies with much larger margins so that they would fit the common double-crown (30in x 20in) format used on most advertising sites throughout London. *London Transport Museum*

Nothing is paid for the space occupied, clear evidence that they are welcome. They were the first maps to be shown in London streets, opposite stopping places, and they hang in the class-rooms or corridors of 1,600 schools.

Anticipating the Enquiry
Signs – At one time it was considered sufficient to say 'Cars stop here.' The present practice is to supplement this informa-tion: to name the places served and the car numbers for them. This is the kind of service that the public appreciate.

In these days of intense movement the street is more and more a place for advertising travel. The town crier has come back. But his appeal is less strident, more subtle. He employs the skill of the artist and the printer. He puts a sign here, in a strategic position, to catch the eye of the tired pedestrian. At night he lights up the sign. At a busy junction he puts a map. Maps are puzzles to some people still, so on it he draws a direction arrow and against it he writes 'YOU ARE HERE.' And somewhere else he puts a picture, just where crowds collect.

Pocket maps and leaflets are means by which the story can be told in detail. The best agents for maps and leaflets are inspectors and regulators. Maps and leaflets are the trump card of the zealous official. When dear old ladies have been told over and over again the times of all the last cars, when the officials' patience is nigh exhausted, they can produce the maps and leaflets like manna in the desert. The best plan is to deliver the goods early in the dialogue. They make a better impression and have the qualities of soothing syrup. And the official maintains for the Tramways its reputation for alertness and obliging manners.

We cannot repeat the miracle of pre-war days and sell for a penny a book whose pages ran to 186. Some of you will remember that book. Instead we offer a series of leaflets for nothing, leaflets that may be had for the asking. Last year we had a good arrangement with the schools. On the eve of the summer holidays the teachers handed illustrated leaflets to 61,000 children, and this year the plan will be repeated on a two-fold scale.

The tramway poles, which carried the overhead wires, were ideal places on which to display the corporation's posters. This photograph shows Marsden Lea's poster of Hampstead still on display five months after it was issued in May 1929.
London Transport Museum

'See London'
Here is a wide field to cultivate. The children of today will be your grown-up passengers tomorrow. At one school in Greenwich the headmaster asked how many boys aged from 7 to 10 had been to London proper, that is, across the bridge.

There were 130 boys. How many do you think had crossed the Thames at Blackfriars, Westminster or Waterloo? Only 50: 50 out of 130. And this will interest you men of North London. An Inspector of LCC schools made this discovery. The number of Islington children who had seen the Thames was only one in three. Think of that when you run from The Angel to the Thames bank in 12 minutes.

When the advertisement has been planned, designed and printed, there remains the all-important question of distribution and display. This is where the staff can be of great help. A torn poster in the street, an out-of-date notice in the car, a sign not switched on at night – these are the bugbears of outdoor advertising. They are like dirty tunics and boots on the Army parade ground – but in my opinion the effect is a hundred times worse. Report then, immediately, any of the following:

> *Damaged poster*
> *Dirty destination posters, farebills and timebills*
> *Signs that are not lighted.*

Passengers write to the offices and say they cannot obtain a map. Conductors should politely refer applicants to inspectors and regulators. To the latter we say: Keep a large enough supply. Renew it when it is low. Keep all maps and leaflets clean, just as clean as they come from the printers. Bins at regulators' points have boxes for holding maps and so on, nice wallets are provided for carrying them. Offer copies to everyone not familiar with tramway facilities. Remember that every bit of printed paper costs money. Remember also that it is a potential earner of revenue and goodwill.

Who are the best publicity agents?
Why am I telling you all this? How do we come into it? The answer is that the publicity of the Tramways is not the responsibility of the Head Office alone. It is the responsibility of each one of us, especially those who come in contact with the public. The publicity efforts of Head Office are as nothing compared with the influence that can be exerted by yourselves. The best publicity Agents of the Tramways are the motorman, conductor, the inspector and regulator, men in a position every minute of the day to advertise the system by word deed and bearing.

Finally, if the shops in Holloway Road were destroyed tonight many of the owners would still possess a very valuable asset. That of goodwill – the outcome of fair dealing and courteous attention. They say that Mr. So-and-So never gives short weight, that his assistants are as polite to the woman who spends a penny as to the one who spends a shilling. The goodwill of the LCC Tramways is of enormous value. Here in North London you have helped to build that goodwill. With you lies the power to preserve it and increase it.

Following on from the success of these posters by the Central School of Arts and Crafts, LCCT began to commission posters designed by other artists and advertising agencies, in particular Ralph & Brown studios whose first poster appeared in 1925. From the evidence of the surviving posters it would appear that the years 1925 to 1927 were a turning point in the commissioning policy of the tramways. In 1925 the Central School students designed all but one poster, but by 1926 less than half are attributed to the Central School, and some or all of these may have been designed in 1925. In 1927 not one is attributed to the School.

The tramways never produced more than about 12 pictorial posters a year and so could not compete in numbers with those produced by the Underground Group. And although, on the whole, the artists they employed never reached such international fame as did many of those employed by the Underground, the overall quality of their posters remained very high.

As has already been noted, London trams were suffering from competition from the motorbuses. The trams were seen as old fashioned, uncomfortable and working class compared to the new modern and more luxurious motor bus. There was some truth in this and one of the aims of the posters was to promote the new luxury tramcars being introduced partly in response to the competition provided by the motorbus. As a result a relatively large number of these posters advertised these new vehicles. Indeed compared to the posters issued by the Underground Group where there are very few posters even showing an Underground train, tram or bus even as incidental detail in the poster, a much higher proportion of the LCCT posters portrayed the council's vehicles and in doing so often made them seem modern, stylish and dynamic. After all, the purpose of the LCCT posters was to promote travel by tram.

In looking back over these posters a clear progression can be seen from the early black and white designs of 1924 through the colour posters also designed by students from the Central through to those designed by advertising agencies and professional commercial artists. Unlike the Underground posters where many of the same artists continued to design posters throughout the interwar years, the artists employed by the LCC changed to the extent that a completely different set of artists and agencies designed the later posters from those designing the earlier posters up to 1926. This must have been a conscious decision since most of the artists employed in the early years were still working throughout this period, with some becoming well known names in artistic circles. Most artists designed only one or two posters, with a small number designing more. The one notable exception was Peter Brown of the Ralph and Brown studios. He designed over 20 posters, making him the most prolific of the LCC's artists by far.

In just 13 years many changes can be seen not just in the style but also in the choice of subjects portrayed in the posters. The latter may reflect the changes in the tramways' services themselves with the introduction of the 1/- all day and 6d tourist tickets, the development of the more luxurious Pullman tram and the re-opening of the enlarged Kingsway tunnel. However, it is unfortunate that just as quickly as they appeared on the London street scene in 1932 these fine examples of poster art disappeared in 1933 when the council's tramways were merged into the newly formed London Passenger Transport Board. The LPTB under Frank Pick continued to issue many very fine examples of poster art, but these were in the format and style of the Underground poster and quite different from the LCCT's own distinctive poster style. As a result the LCCT poster has been largely overshadowed and forgotten since the last one was issued over 75 years ago.

The LCC's tram shelters could be found throughout their tram network. Large or small, they made the perfect place to display posters. This picture of the shelter at Scrubs Lane, taken in August 1933, was one of many taken by the London Passenger Transport Board to record its new assets. The posters issued in March and May of that year would soon be taken down to be replaced by London Transport's own advertising. *London Transport Museum*

THE FIRST POSTERS

This first set of posters in black and white, and designed by students at the Central School of Arts and Crafts, were the only ones to carry the LCC's coat of arms. However, the corporate style did not extend to the hand-drawn serif lettering which varied from poster to poster. The unusual size of $28\frac{1}{2}$ x $14\frac{1}{4}$in was to become the LCC Tramways' norm, although later posters also appeared in larger sizes.

To Kenwood
(artwork)
S M White, 1922

Lawn Tennis at Wimbledon
Frank P Restall, 1922

This was the only pictorial poster issued by the LCCT to advertise this major sporting event.

Under Cover all the Way
F W C Farleigh, 1922

Farleigh's experiments in wood engraving in 1921 may have enabled him to produce such a striking design in black and white for this poster.

Bostall Woods
Miss Hammond, 1922

Epping Forest
F W C Farleigh, 1922

Cricket at the Oval
Frank P Restall, 1922

This design by Restall was adapted and re-used several times both for further posters and leaflets listing cricket fixtures in the 1930s.

Late Theatre services by Tramway (artwork)
Margaret Curtis
Haythorne, 1922

Christmas Shopping
F W C Farleigh, 1922

Farleigh's view of London
from the rooftop of
County Hall, then the
home of the LCC, takes
great licence with the
actual geography,
compressing as it does
many of London's
landmarks from the
Houses of Parliament
on the left to St Paul's
on the right. Double
deck trams cross the
bridges and run along
the Embankment, whilst
single deck trams
disappear into Kingsway
Tunnel. Otherwise the
streets are empty. On a
hill in the background is
a church, possibly that of
Harrow-on-the-Hill.

**Dull Days Made Bright in
the Museums**
Margaret Curtis
Haythorne, 1922

Happy Days at the Zoo
Muriel Blomfield
Jackson, 1922

**The Pantomime – Travel
by Tram**
Edward G Patterson,
1922

Children's Fares
Dorothy Bedford, 1923

LONDON'S PARKS

Although many Londoners lived close to one of London's numerous parks, the Tramways department were keen to encourage them to discover those further away from home by advertising their delights not just in the vicinity of the park but throughout London. Many of the parks were owned by the LCC, whose parks department would have encouraged the tramways to promote them.

Battersea Park
(artwork)
Faith Gaskell, 1928

Gaskell's design shows the importance of using the same or complementary style of lettering to create an eye catching poster with the lettering being of equal importance as the image in creating the overall effect of the poster.

Brockwell Park

(artwork for 60in x 40in poster)
G Fitzgerald, 1929

The LCC acquired Brockwell Park in 1891 and it opened to the public the following year. It is now home to the lively Lambeth Country Fair, which uniquely combines the events of a traditional English country show, with the urban attractions that Lambeth has to offer.

The poster below, with the little girl peering off to the left, appears to have no focal point. The reason for this is that the poster was crudely adapted to this size by cropping the left hand side of the image, creating a less than satisfactory result. As can be seen, the original design for the 4-sheet poster has a clear focal point to which the viewer and girl are both looking and is much more successful.

Brockwell Park

G Fitzgerald, 1929

Battersea Park
(artwork for 60in x 40in poster)
A Murray, 1933

Battersea Park on the South Bank of the
Thames, has hosted many important
events including the first exhibition
game of football played under the rules
of the Football Association. Today a
haven of peace and tranquility, it is hard
to believe that it is only minutes away
from the hustle and bustle of Sloane
Square and the Kings Road.

Battersea Park

The artwork for the 4-sheet poster was also successfully adapted by the artist by extending the image at the top and bottom to create an even more successful design for the smaller 28½in x 14¼in poster.

Chrysanthemum Show – Victoria Park
(artwork and detail)
R G Praill, 1927

Note how the colours of the flowers have
been reversed from the artwork to the
finished poster. It was not felt necessary
for the artist to produce another artwork
since notes for the printer would achieve
the same effect.

Chrysanthemum Show – Victoria Park
R G Praill, 1927

Chrysanthemum Show – Battersea Park
Ralph and Brown Studios, 1931

Hyde Park
René Blair, 1930

Blair's posters often convey a rather traditional, old-fashioned look. Although this view of boating on the Serpentine is amongst his best work for the LCCT, its effect is deadened by the rather heavy and sombre lettering.

LONDON'S TRAMWAYS

HYDE PARK
PULLMAN TRAMS
TO WEST END
TOTTENHAM
COURT Rᴰ
BLOOMSBURY
HOLBORN

Kew in Autumn
Leslie Porter, 1925

The Royal Botanical Gardens, Kew, which celebrated its 250th anniversary in 2009, is located between Richmond and Kew. It is one of the world's leading botanic gardens and a global centre of plant science.

This delightful poster was the only one issued by the LCCT to advertise Kew Gardens. This was probably because it could only be reached via one LCCT service compared with the many routes to Battersea, Brockwell or Victoria parks.

Ruskin Park
Frank P Restall, 1923

St James's Park

St James's Park is variously spelt with
and without the final 's' and sometimes,
as in this first poster, without either
the apostrophe or the 's'. St James's
Park lies at the very heart of London.
Its 58 acres serve as a tranquil oasis
for London's office workers. It is also
a major destination for tourists as it
is hemmed in by Horseguards Parade,
Buckingham Palace and The Mall with
all their associated ceremonial and
political events.

St James Park
F Roberts Johnson, 1931

The bird most closely associated with
St James's Park is the pelican, so it is
surprising that this attractive modernist
image by Johnson shows just a duck
swimming through the water, whilst
another poster by Danvers shows what
appears to be a cormorant eating fish.

LONDON'S TRAMWAYS

ST. JAMES PARK
TRAM SERVICES
FROM ALL PARTS TO
WESTMINSTER & VICTORIA

St James' Park
V L Danvers, 1926

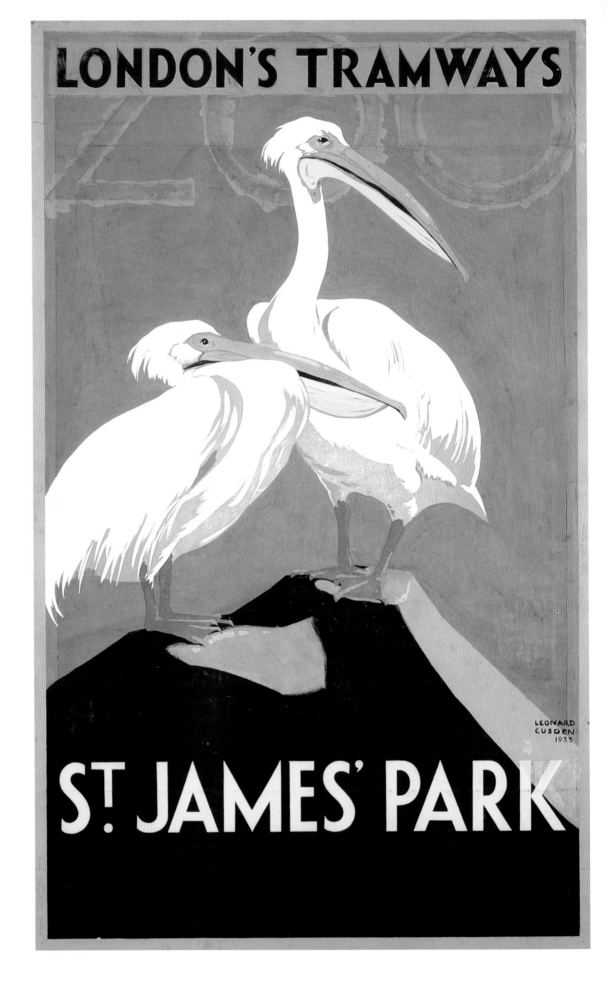

St James' Park
Leonard Cusden, 1933

St James' Park
opposite
(artwork)
Leonard Cusden, 1933

The artist originally intended this poster to advertise the Zoo, as can be seen from the lettering which he has overpainted at the top of the poster. It is not known if this was a mistake on the part of the artist or a change in the brief as the design could work equally well for either destination.

St James Park
Ralph and Brown Studios, 1928

St James Park
W Gale Harris, 1929

The artist does not show the usual views along the park to Horseguards or Buckingham Palace but instead has chosen to frame the towers of Westminster Abbey between the park's trees as it appears over the roof tops of the surrounding buildings.

LONDON'S TRAMWAYS

ST JAMES PARK

BY SERVICES 33,35
VIA THE ANGEL
AND BLOOMSBURY

St James' Park
W Langlands, 1933

Looking at the eight posters advertising St James's it is clear that the LCCT did not enforce a corporate style in its typography. There are almost as many styles of lettering in the heading 'London's Tramways' as there are posters. This alone, even without the evidence of the original artwork, is clear proof that the lettering was done by the artist.

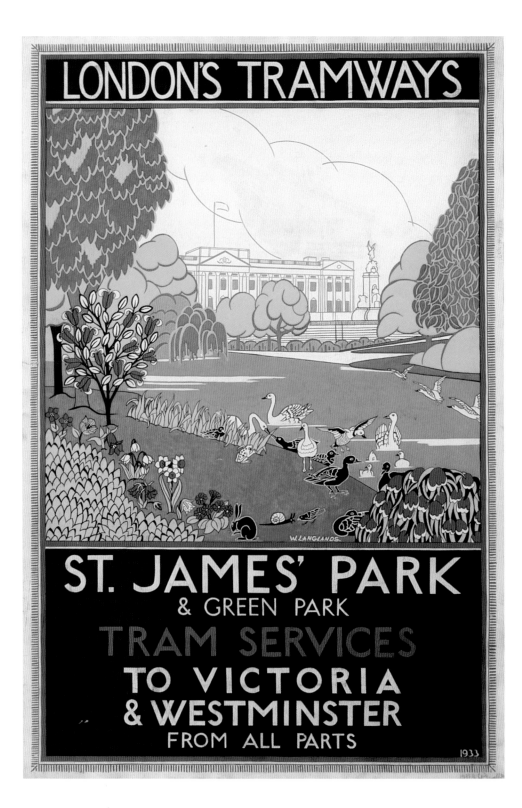

St James' Park
Frederica Graham, 1925

This poster clearly shows the park in its autumn splendour in the hope of encouraging more visitors to enjoy the park at this quieter time of the year.

LONDON'S TRAMWAYS

ST. JAMES' PARK
TO WESTMINSTER OR
VICTORIA BY TRAM

DESIGNED AT THE LCC CENTRAL SCHOOL OF ARTS AND CRAFTS

THE ZOO

Soon after being opened to the public in 1847 London Zoo quickly became one of London's biggest tourist attractions. The LCC wanted its trams to capture a significant share of this market and like the Underground issued an annual poster to promote its services to the Zoo, the one exception being 1923. Over the years the zoo has undergone significant changes. In the 1990s it was threatened with closure, due to lack of funds and the public attitude towards animals being kept in captivity. However, when it was announced that London Zoo would close in 1991, a swell of public support in visitors and donations allowed it to continue its work, and take on the huge task of creating environments that offer the animals a better lifestyle.

London Zoo was always a popular destination for days out and the LCCT wanted its share of this important market. So just like the Underground, which issued posters each year promoting travel by its services to the Zoo, the LCC also issued an annual poster encouraging Londoners to travel by tram. The one exception was 1923, when no poster was issued.

Camden Town for the Zoo
Mary I Wright, 1924

32

Camden Town for the Zoo
F W C Farleigh, 1925

The Zoo – Parrots
(artwork)
Van Jones, 1927

Many artworks would have
instructions added to aid the printer,
either by the artist or from the
tramways own publicity department
which would have to approve the
designs. On this design by Van
Jones, the many notes indicate
changes to the text and style
of lettering, and the necessary
changes that must be made so that
the design can be used for both the
60in x 40in and the 28½ x 14¼in
formats. When a double crown
format was required the 4-sheet was
not scaled down; it was probably
cheaper to use the smaller artwork
and enlarge the border rather than
to re-draw the artwork for the
smaller scale.

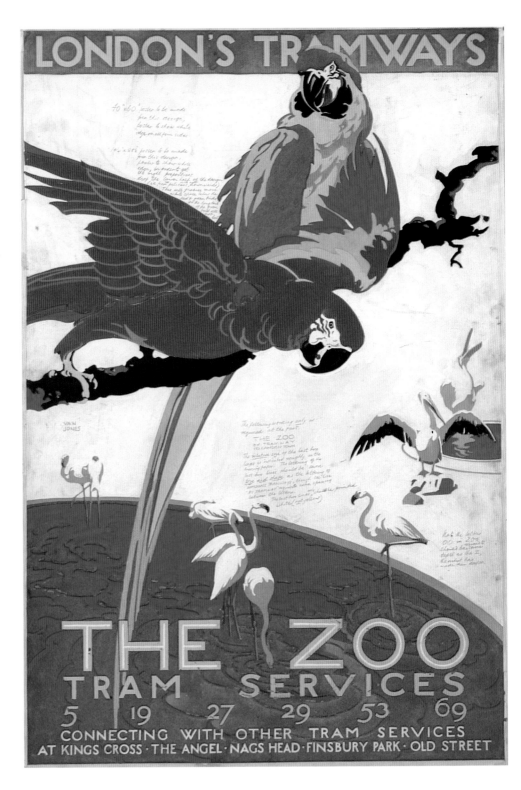

The Zoo – Parrots
Van Jones, 1927

The Zoo – Parrots
Lawson Wood, 1932

The Zoo – Monkeys
(artwork)
Edmunds, 1928

Here the artist has incorrectly
spelt Camden Town.

The Zoo – Giraffe
opposite
(artwork)
M K Mountain, 1931

The Zoo – Giraffes
(artwork)
Oliver Burridge, 1926

The Zoo – Toucans
Tony Castle, 1929

The bills of these toucans are almost as
long as their bodies, and the designer
uses them to maximum effect to create a
brilliant composition in this bold poster.

The Zoo – Lion cub
M K Mountain, 1930

The Zoo – Flamingoes
Frank Marsden Lea, 1932

The Zoo – Leopard
(artwork)
M K Mountain, 1930

43

TOURIST LONDON

It was very obvious to the managers of both the Underground and the tramways that Londoners did not know their own city and many of the posters issued by both organisations aimed to address this problem.

Caledonian Market
Edward G Patterson, 1923

This was the first colour poster to be issued by the LCC Tramways.

LONDON'S TRAMWAYS

CALEDONIAN MARKET
EVERY FRIDAY
CALEDONIAN ROAD
AND CAMDEN ROAD
TRAMWAY SERVICES

Dickens' London – The Borough
Miss I Jephson, 1923

The Borough is home to the The George, the last remaining galleried inn in London. It was established in the medieval period and is mentioned in Charles Dickens's Little Dorrit. It is still used as a public house, but is now protected and owned by the National Trust.

LONDON'S TRAMWAYS

DICKENS' LONDON THE BOROUGH

DESIGNED AT THE L.C.C. CENTRAL SCHOOL OF ARTS & CRAFTS.

WATERLOW & SONS LIMITED LONDON DUNSTABLE & WATFORD

Westminster Abbey
G M Norris, 1926

With around only 12 pictorial posters
issued each year it seems extravagant
of the LCCT to commission two artists to
paint the same subject in one year, yet
this was one of two posters advertising
Westminster Abbey in 1926.

LONDON'S TRAMWAYS

WESTMINSTER ABBEY
TRAM SERVICES 33·35
TO VICTORIA EMBANKMENT
VIA THE ANGEL & BLOOMSBURY

London's Tramways to Embankment
Freda Beard, 1928.

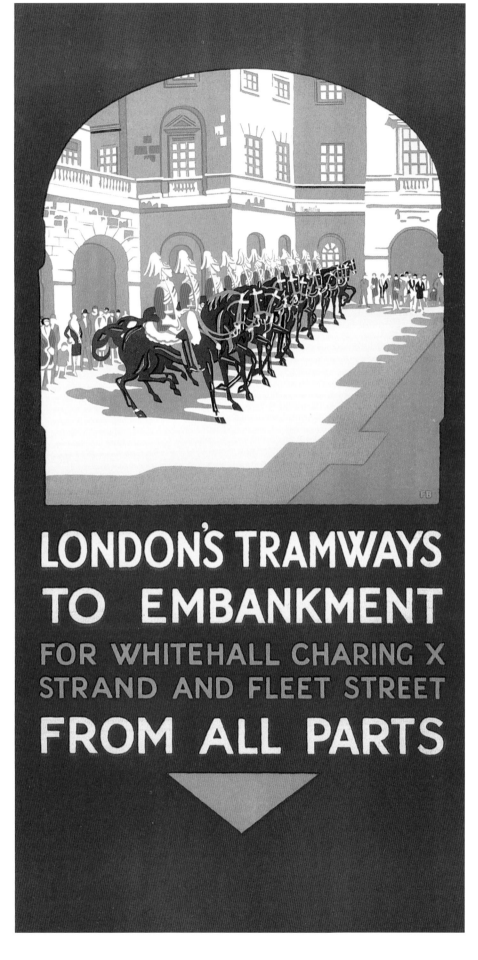

Modern London
J G Rennie, 1932

This poster picks out some of the more
interesting modern buildings that could
be found in central London by travelling
on the Embankment and Kingsway tram
services which are shown on the central
map. The only building shown to the
south of the river is the council's own
County Hall which was opened by King
George V in 1922.

See More of London – Ride at Will for 1/-
G E Butler, 1933

This rather old fashioned style poster promotes many of central London's better known landmarks and rather surprisingly Brockwell Park, all of which could be reached cheaply using the tramways 1/- Ride at Will ticket.

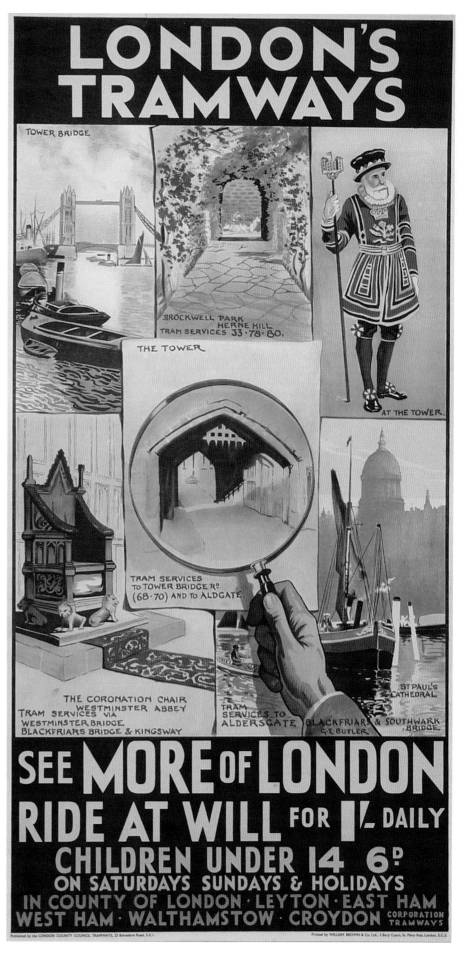

THE CITY AND THE WEST END

London's tramways, so much a feature of London, never really penetrated into the heart of the City or West End except for the one route through the Kingsway Tunnel. This did not stop them promoting central London attractions, even though they could not bring passengers as close to most of their passengers' destinations as the competing Underground or buses.

By Tramway to Central London for Shops and Theatres
J L Carstairs, 1927

BY TRAMWAY
TO CENTRAL LONDON
FOR
SHOPS
AND
THEATRES
A WEST-END GUIDE IS ISSUED FREE
APPLY TO ANY INSPECTOR OR REGULATOR

For the City
Tony Castle, 1928

Whether it is the white lettering on black, or the way the tram is drawn crossing Southwark Bridge, this poster has a rather old-fashioned and staid look to it, suggesting nothing of the movement and speed shown in many of the other posters.

London's Tramways to Central London
H McCready, 1930

This poster gives the impression of movement and speed as trams are pulled into the centre of London, here represented by a star or the sun. Whilst it is true that trams did reach Tottenham Court Road they did not run along it, as they only reached its most northern tip where it joined the Euston Road.

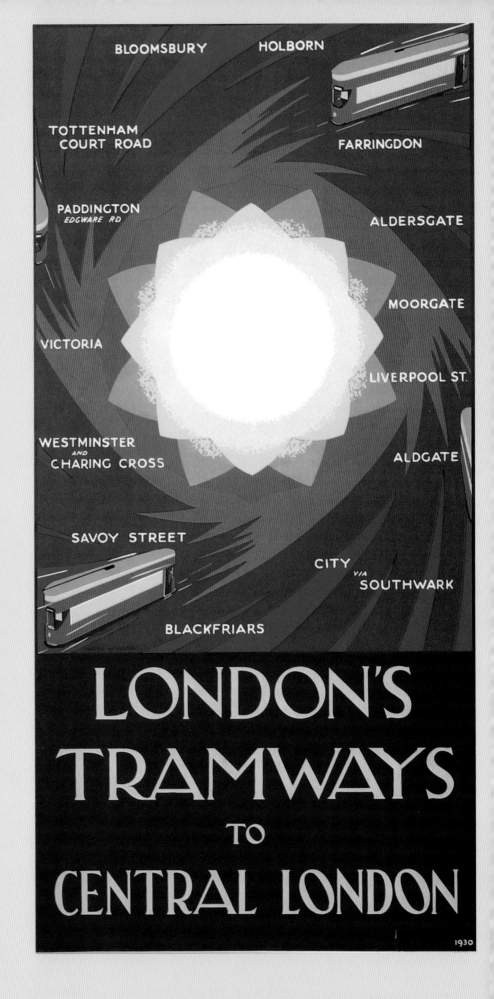

Southwark Bridge – the New Tramway Connection with the City
Oliver Burridge, 1925

Because of political resistance, trams never penetrated into the heart of the City but in 1925 an extension was built across Southwark Bridge.

LONDON'S TRAMWAYS

SOUTHWARK BRIDGE
THE NEW TRAMWAY CONNECTION WITH THE CITY

DESIGNED AT THE L.C.C. CENTRAL SCHOOL OF ARTS AND CRAFTS

WATERLOW & SONS LIMITED, LONDON, DUNSTABLE & WATFORD.

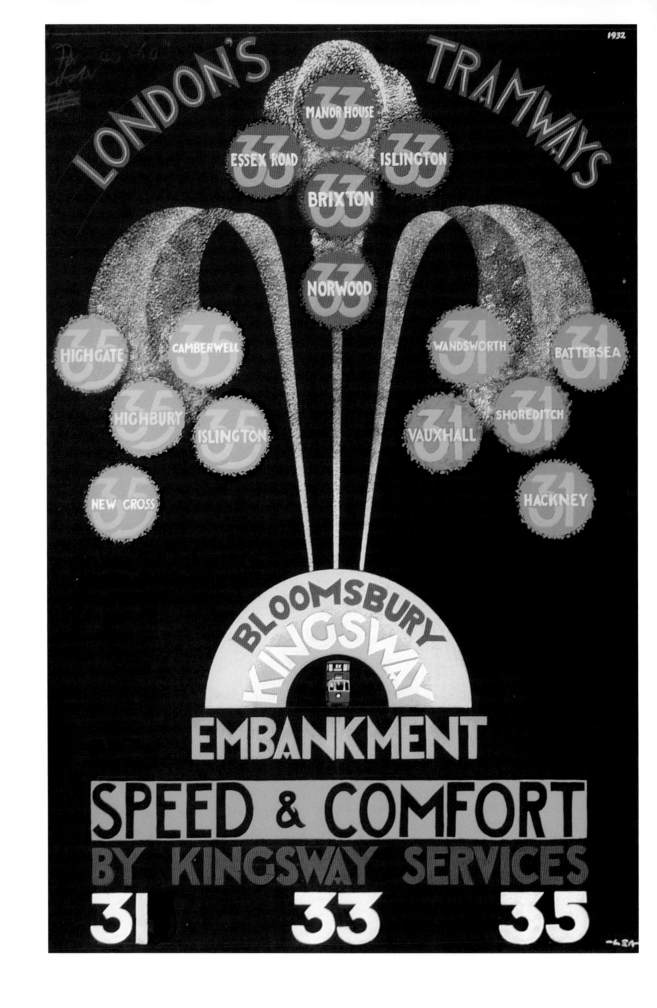

ALONG THE EMBANKMENT AND THROUGH THE SUBWAY

With its riverside location and its importance in linking the tramway networks north and south of the river, the Embankment and the Kingsway subway became popular subjects for the poster artists.

These two posters are strikingly similar in design. The tram emerging out of the tunnel under a blaze of fireworks suggests a somewhat festive air, but it is not thought that the poster was advertising any particular event. It is also surprising that the LCC approved them as they incorrectly portray the Kingsway Subway as single track.

Embankment – Speed and Comfort
opposite
Frank Marsden Lea, 1932

Speed & Comfort by Kingsway Services
Starr, 1932

To Victoria Embankment by Tramway
Ralph and Brown Studios, 1928

During the reconstruction of Piccadilly Circus station, Eros was removed to the Embankment Gardens for a number of years.

**Victoria Embankment for the
West End and City**
Ralph and Brown Studios, 1929

Victoria Embankment
R F Fordred, 1932

Victoria Embankment
Monica Rawlins, 1926

The Embankment was one of the busiest routes on the tramway system with 'always a car in sight' so '400 cars an hour at high tide' or rush hour was no idle boast. The trams are portrayed in the traditional purple lake and primrose livery, which later that year began to be replaced as part of the 'Pullmanisation programme'.

Victoria Embankment
Frank Marsden Lea, 1931

London's Tramways
Anonymous, 1930

**To Theatreland by London's
Tramways**
(artwork)
P Irwin Brown (of Leigh Breton
Studios), 1927

The notes written all over this
original design for the 60in x
40in version of the poster clearly
illustrate their role in the process of
producing a poster. From this heavily
annotated artwork, a lithographic
artist at the printers would redraw
the picture, making any necessary
alterations, on to a plate ready to be
printed. The finished poster (here
the smaller 28½ x 14¼in version)
shows some of the changes that
were made. *This design was also
used on the cover of leaflets as part
of a co-ordinated campaign.*

London's Tramways to the West End
P Irwin Brown (of Leigh Breton Studios)
1927

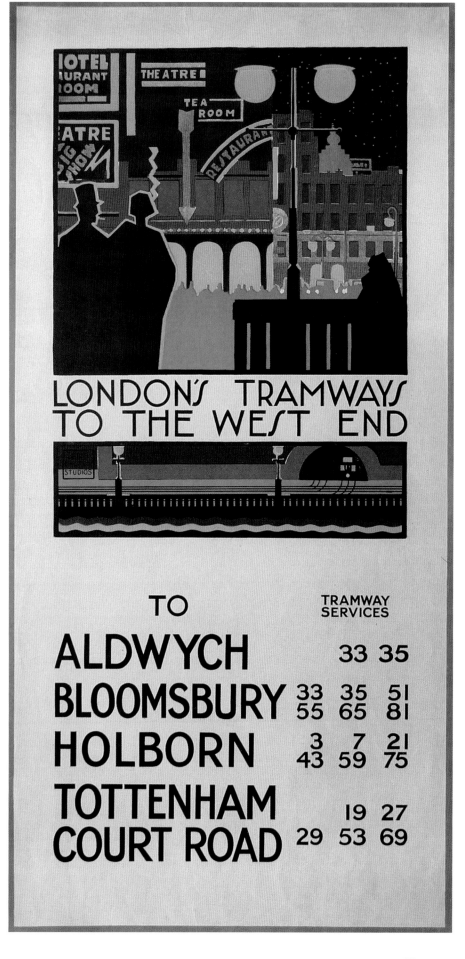

Late Theatre services by Tramway
F W C Farleigh, 1922

Farleigh's bright and colourful poster, in which elegantly dressed passengers stream forth from the tram gives the impression that trams actually penetrated into the West End when in fact they only reached Euston Road from the north, Kingsway to the east and the Embankment and Victoria Station from the south.

LONDON'S TRAMWAYS

THEATRE LAND LATE SERVICES BY TRAMWAY

DESIGNED AT THE L.C.C. CENTRAL SCHOOL OF ARTS AND CRAFTS

VINCENT BROOKS DAY & SON LTD Lith London W.C.2.

64

Our Way to the Party
Maud Klein, 1924

MUSEUMS

With London's wide choice of museums and art galleries it is not known why the LCCT decided to concentrate their poster advertising on just a few museums. Several other museums and galleries were equally if not better served by the corporation's trams.

The Guildhall Art Gallery and Museum
Leslie Abbott, 1928

Old Furniture at the Geffrye Museum
Francis Howard Spear, 1924

The Geffrye Museum was opened by the
LCC in 1914. Thus this poster, with its
birdseye view of trams running along the
front of the museum, had the benefit in
the council's eye of advertising two of
their undertakings for the price of one.

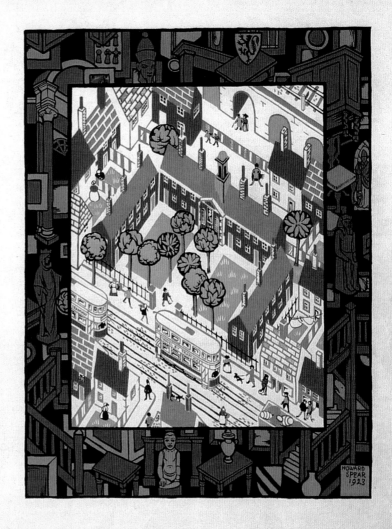

Tate Gallery
Lance Cattermole, 1925

Whilst Lance Cattermole's poster clearly shows the well known facade of the Tate Gallery, now Tate Britain, Tony Castle's poster required a more generic image which at first glance could apply to both galleries.

LONDON'S TRAMWAYS

TATE GALLERY
ALL TRAM SERVICES
TO VICTORIA
ALIGHT AT GROSVENOR RD.

DESIGNED AT THE L.C.C. CENTRAL SCHOOL OF ARTS AND CRAFTS

Tate Gallery – National Gallery
Tony Castle, 1927

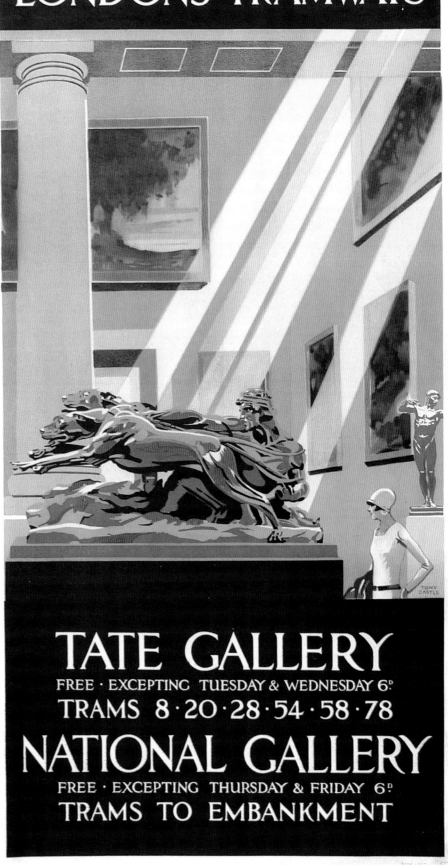

THE THAMES

Two very different aspects of the
Thames are shown in these posters
– that of a working river with its steam
tugs and sailing barges, and also as
a place for relaxation on, in or by the
water.

By Tram to the Embankment
Herbert Rooke, 1924

Greenwich Beach and Pier
Morris Kestelman, 1925

In the 1920s and 30s the beach at
Greenwich, with its imported sand, was
popular with many Londoners who could
not afford the time or money to go to the
sea. Apart from this temporary beach,
the Thames below London was still
primarily a working river. Kestelman,
who was a student at the Central School
of Arts and Crafts when he designed this
poster, returned to the school in 1951 to
become its Head of Fine Art until 1971.

The Thames at Hammersmith and Putney
Ralph and Brown Studios, 1929

Putney is well known for its picturesque location on the Thames and its association with the Oxford and Cambridge boat race which originated from an idea between two schoolfriends who attended the Universities. The first challenge was set in 1829 and it has now become an annual fixture in the international sporting calendar. Spectators line the banks of the Thames from Putney to Mortlake to catch the best view.

LONDON'S TRAMWAYS

PUTNEY BRIDGE
AND
FULHAM CHURCH

THE THAMES AT HAMMERSMITH AND
PUTNEY
TRAM SERVICES 26 28 30 89

Putney for River and Health
R F Fordred, 1933

Although the trams were always considered to be a working class form of transport, much more so than the buses and Underground, in this and other posters the LCC depicted people as elegant and fashionable. In selling London to Londoners the posters appealed to their aspirations rather than reminded them of the grime and hardship of everyday life. Here the council's trams are the only vehicles to be seen running over Putney Bridge.

The River at Putney
Herbert Rooke, 1924

Strand on the Green
Margaret Curtis Haythorne, 1924

EPPING FOREST TO WIMBLEDON COMMON

Since at least the nineteenth century Londoners have been concerned about the ever increasing urban sprawl and loss of countryside. Whether saved by Act of Parliament or bought by the LCC, London is fortunate to have so many suburban open spaces providing a green lung for its inhabitants.

Putney Heath
Tony Castle, 1927

The LCC was always keen to encourage Londoners to enjoy the benefits and delights of its many open spaces. Putney Heath and Wimbledon Common, with its 1,140 acres and over 16 miles of rides, managed to resist the urban sprawl of Putney, Wimbledon and Kingston-upon-Thames. The commons, which are often used by riders, are also patrolled by Rangers who are often on horseback and are a welcome attraction in themselves as well as offering safety and protection to visitors.

LONDON'S TRAMWAYS

PUTNEY HEATH
TRAM SERVICES · 26 · 28 · 30
WIMBLEDON
TRAM SERVICES · 2 · 4

Streatham Common and the Rookery
Tony Castle, 1927

The Rookery is a formally-landscaped garden which opened to the public in 1913. It was formerly known as the Streatham Spa, due to the local spring water famous for its medicinal and healing properties, and was in the grounds of a large house called `The Rookery'. When the spa was under threat of closure local residents campaigned to save it and it is now used as an open air theatre in the summer months.

To Purley
Agnes D Gower, 1926

In 1926 Purley was very much at the edge of suburban London, where it bordered what still remained of Surrey's countryside. To get there the trams ran through Croydon, but this was never advertised on the company's posters – maybe because the corporation of Croydon operated its own tram system.

Wimbledon Common
G W Widmer, 1923

The Windmill, built in 1817, remains the most prominent feature of the common. It was originally saved in the 1890s by a public appeal and opened as a museum in 1976. The conservation of the common is of foremost importance and the great open space, woodland and many ponds are a draw for many local people, giving it a real feel of the countryside. Even with 10,000 visitors on an average weekend it is still possible to enjoy peace and solitude here.

Eltham and Castlewood
Leslie Porter, 1926

This view shows Severndroog Castle, which was a folly built in 1784 to commemorate the capture of the pirate fortress of Severndroog in India. The design was used to advertise two different combinations of destinations. Although the main image does not change, the title of the picture has been removed and for no apparent reason the artist's signature has also been altered as has the style of lettering. The fact that the reference to the poster being designed at the LCC Central School of Arts and Crafts has also been removed clearly shows that the absence of this wording on some of the earlier posters does not necessarily mean that they were not designed by the school's students.

80

Castlewood
Leslie Porter, 1926

To Wimbledon (Queensmere)
Leslie Porter, 1926

Bostall Woods
R P Sleeman, 1931

Epping Forest
(artwork)
Mary I Wright, 1928

Epping Forest
opposite
Tony Castle, 1926

In 1878 an act of Parliament
saved Epping Forest from
development. At almost 6,000
acres it remains London's
largest open space. These four
posters show two very different
aspects of the Forest, as a
haven for wildlife and also as
a place to enjoy the fun of the
fairground.

LONDON'S TRAMWAYS

EPPING FOREST
TRAM SERVICES
55 & 81   57   61
FROM BLOOMSBURY   LIVERPOOL ST.   ALDGATE
FROM SOUTH LONDON : 33 35 CHANGE AT BLOOMSBURY

Epping Forest
G S Brien and F Sherwin (Hobo Bros), 1929

Epping Forest
P Irwin Brown (Ralph and Brown Studios),
1930

GREENWICH PARK

Greenwich, which sits on the Thames, is famous for its naval and maritime connections and at first it was this riverside aspect that the tramways chose to promote through their posters. However, from 1926, the LCCT posters turned their back on the river to focus on the Royal Park and deer which were introduced by Henry VII.

Greenwich Park
(artwork)
R P Sleeman, 1931

Greenwich
Leslie Porter, 1926

Greenwich Park
Ralph and Brown Studios, 1929

Greenwich Park
Frank Marsden Lea, 1932

HAMPSTEAD AND KENWOOD

Well served by the council's trams,
the open spaces of Kenwood and
Hampstead were the main destinations
in north London to appear on the
tramways' posters.

Hampstead Heath and Ken Wood
Frank Marsden Lea, 1929

Hampstead Heath and Parliament Hill
(artwork)
Lance Cattermole, 1933

Although the grounds had been bought for Londoners in 1922, Kenwood House with its panoramic views over London was not given to the nation until 1927. Bereft of its original fittings it was soon to house the art gallery which is advertised on the poster. The gallery is of international importance, including works such as 'The Guitar Player' by Johannes Vermeer and a self portrait by Rembrandt.

Hampstead Heath, Ken Wood and Parliament Hill
A Murray, 1931

Hampstead Heath and Parliament Hill
R F Fordred, 1933

This poster was designed as a double crown (30 x 20in) poster, which was unusual for the LCCT, rather than as the smaller 28½ x 14¼in format with larger margins added.

KEN WOOD
Showing the Art Gallery
Open Wednesdays & Fridays
1/- — other days FREE.

R·F·FORDRED 1933

HAMPSTEAD HEATH
& PARLIAMENT HILL

Kenwood and Hampstead Heath
(artwork)
Leslie Carr, 1926

As was the case with several of the posters, this design was also used on the cover of the tramway map for the same year.

Ken Wood and Hampstead Heath
Ralph and Brown Studios, 1928

Ken Wood & Highgate Ponds
Van Jones, 1927

The ponds on Hampstead Heath are open all year round, with many dedicated swimmers braving the water on Christmas day. The two most attractive ponds are still strictly divided between men and women, and, partly due to the no mobile phones policy, offer a tranquil haven on a summer's day.

This attractive view resembles more an Austrian or Swiss lake with its high hills towering above it rather than the gentle hills to be found around Highgate ponds. To increase the dramatic effect of the poster, the artist has also greatly enhanced the size of the diving board which dominated the pond.

Highgate
Oliver Burridge, 1924

The contemporary sans serif lettering adds a more modern perspective to this attractive poster in contrast to its portrayal of Highgate as a quiet, almost deserted street with a shopkeeper standing at a doorway waiting for customers. Apart from the tram, which appears to be running without track, conduit or overhead, the only other vehicle is a horse and cart. Even today Highgate remains an area with the feel of a small village, despite being just 5 miles from central London.

Old Hampstead
Frederick Adcock, 1933

Surprisingly, as one of the last posters to be issued by the tramways before they became part of the London Passenger Transport Board, this poster lacks the strong and modern visual imagery to be found in so many of the LCC Tramways posters. Although this was, no doubt, a conscious decision in trying to make the style fit the subject, it makes it sit uneasily with most of the other posters that were issued.

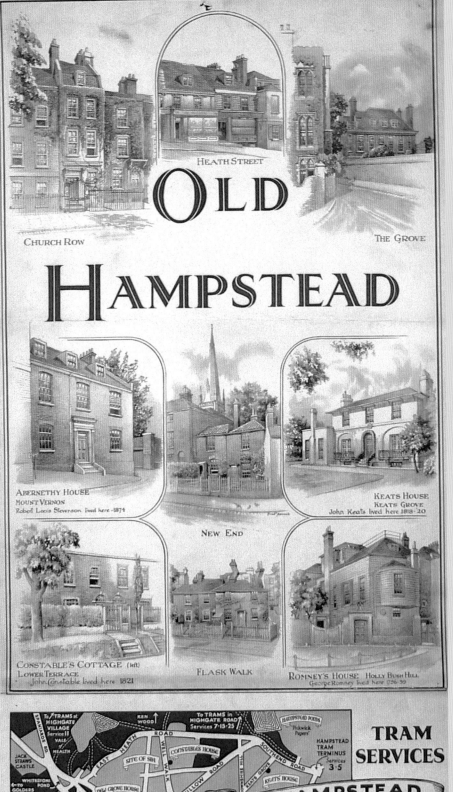

**Tramway Services to Hampstead and
Parliament Hill Fields**
Muriel Jackson, 1924

SPORT

Considering London's vast number and range of sporting venues and the ability of trams to move large numbers of people, the LCCT issued surprisingly few pictorial posters to advertise these events.

To Football by LCC Trams
Ralph and Brown Studios, 1931

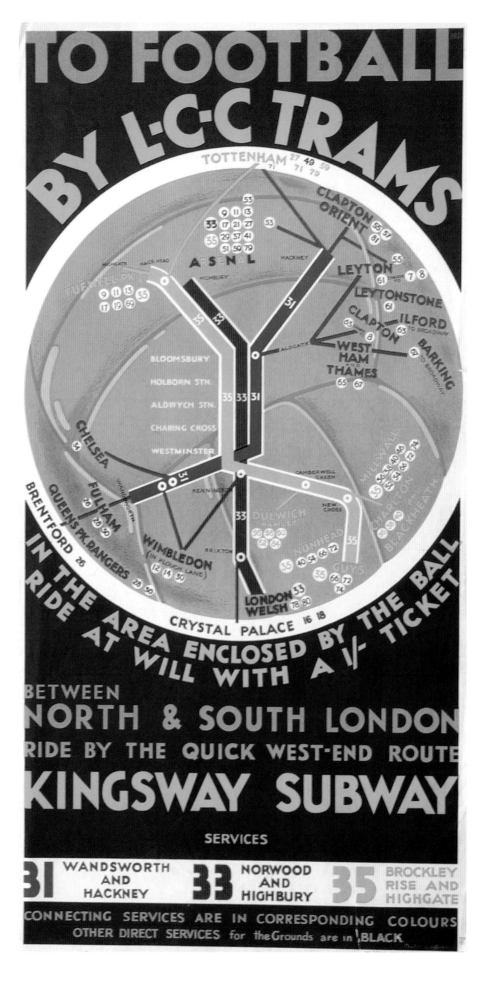

Polo at Avery Hill
Francis Howard Spear, 1923

According to this poster, matches were held three times a week during the season. Considering how few posters were issued by the LCCT, polo might seem to be a rather elitist sport for it to advertise. Avery Hill Park had been owned by the LCC since 1902 and this may have influenced the choice of subject.

Football grounds
Alfred Edmeades Bestall, 1925

Bestall, who produced this poster whilst he was still at the Central School of Arts and Crafts, is better known for writing and illustrating the Rupert Bear stories in the Daily Express.

Your Leg Problem Solved
after Frank P Restall, 1933

Unlike the Underground, whose posters advertised all types of sports fixtures across London, the LCC issued very few posters for sporting events. This was partly because many of the events did not take place in areas served by the LCC's trams, but even when they did the LCC did not seem that concerned to advertise them to the same extent that the Underground did. This double crown poster used Frank Restall's design for his 1922 poster (see page 12). In the 1930s it was reissued several times with slight changes each year.

EXCURSION TICKETS

6d Evening Tourist Tickets by Pullman Tram
Sells Ltd, 1932

The 1d Midday Fare and 1/- Ride at Will Ticket were already popular attempts by the LCC to increase ridership outside the rush hour when in 1932 the corporation introduced the 6d evening tourist ticket to encourage travel after 6pm.

**6d from 6pm daily – Go as you
please in London**
Anonymous, 1933

Round the Clock on LCC Tramways
Edward Walters, 1926

This poster graphically illustrates the different fares and services available at all times of the day and night by LCC trams.

The Road to the Open Spaces
K James, 1932

If Londoners thought that by taking the tram they would be able to reach the open road and countryside they should have read the small print of the poster which states that the fare was 'between suburban and central London', where the former countryside of outer London's parks, commons and forests surrounded by suburbia was the next best thing.

See more of London (plus 4 details)
Ralph and Brown Studios, 1933

This bright and colourful image of London's landmarks was used to promote weekend and holiday travel to four very different parts of London simply by replacing the central image with that of the preferred destination shown enlarged on the poster through the lens of a magnifying glass. The fact that it has no colour makes it stand out even more from the brightness of the rest of the poster.

THE TATE GALLERY

NEAR VAUXHALL BRIDGE

ADMISSION
TUESDAY & WEDNESDAY 6ᵈ · OTHER DAYS FREE

TRAM SERVICES 8·20·28·54·58·78

LONDON'S "PANTRY" BY THE THAMES

TRAM SERVICES TO LONDON BRIDGE
12·14·26·68·70
TO TOWER BRIDGE 68·70
ALSO ALDGATE SERVICES 47·53·61·63·65·67·71

VICTORIA EMBANKMENT GARDENS

TRAM SERVICES VIA
WESTMINSTER·BLACKFRIARS & KINGSWAY

ELTHAM PALACE

TRAM SERVICES 44·46

**Westminster to Bloomsbury,
The Big Penn'orth**
R F Fordred, 1932

This poster advertises the cheap journeys that could be made through the newly re-opened Kingsway subway. Apart from walking, travelling by tram was the cheapest way to travel around London, particularly with their midday fares.

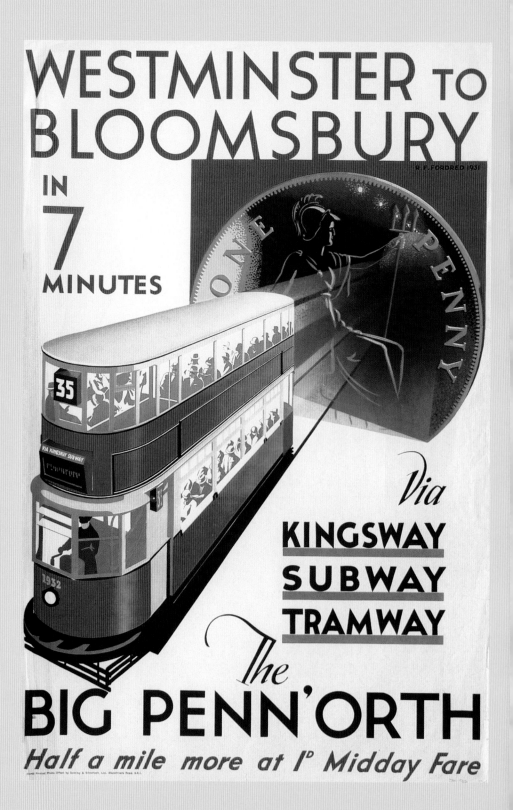

QUALITY OF SERVICE

From 1926 the LCC embarked on a policy of tram refurbishment known as Pullmanisation, resulting in many trams being refurbished with brighter lights, which the LCC claimed allowed passengers to read a newspaper or book in comfort. Seating on both decks was improved but upholstered seating was introduced on the lower deck only.

Ride by LCC Trams for Comfort and Speed
Ralph and Brown Studios, 1929

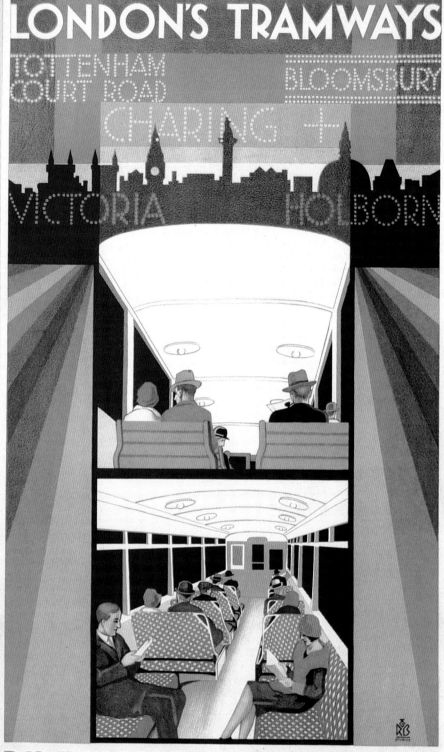

Travel in Comfort by Tram
Frank P Restall, 1923

Travel by Tram for Cover and Comfort
opposite
Francis Howard Spear, 1925

LONDON'S TRAMWAYS

TRAVEL IN COMFORT BY TRAM

DESIGNED AT THE L.C.C. CENTRAL SCHOOL OF ARTS AND CRAFTS

VINCENT BROOKS DAY & SON LTP Lith. London W.C.2

LONDON'S TRAMWAYS

TRAVEL BY TRAM FOR COVER AND COMFORT.

DESIGNED AT THE L·C·C· CENTRAL SCHOOL OF ARTS AND CRAFTS.

Travel Quickly – Read in Comfort
Ralph and Brown Studios, 1927

Pegasus, the winged horse of Greek
mythology, was known for his speed.
Although never used by the LCCT as a logo,
the figure of Pegasus has been adopted by
many other organisations including Mobil
Oil.

For Speedy Travel & Sheltered Comfort
Herbert Kerr Rooke, 1926

CHRISTMAS SHOPPING

From 1926 the Christmas poster was an annual event. Its main purpose was to encourage shoppers to 'shop early' and thus ease the demands on the tramway system. In this it was very successful.

Christmas Shopping – Take an All Day 1/- ticket
Tony Castle, 1926

This poster portraying two fashionable ladies carrying their shopping baskets was obviously aimed at women. Only housewives would be able to take advantage of the all-day 1/- ticket for shopping as most men in the 1920s were still working a 5½ day week.

Shop Early
Freda Beard, 1927

This was the first of the annual Christmas posters to encourage shoppers to shop early and thus relieve some of the pressure on the trams at this busy time of year.

Shop Early
Rowles, 1928

Occasionally, as in this poster, the heading 'London's Tramways' was replaced by other text but the message 'Shop Early' aimed at its women passengers remained the same. According to the LCC, the campaign slogan was so successful it was used every year.

Shop Early – By Pullman Tramcar
René Blair, 1929

This poster contrasts the advantages
of the modern Pullman tramcar, in
which there is plenty of space and the
ride is so smooth that one could read a
paper, with earlier forms of transport.
Before the introduction of the trams and
railways most Londoners would have
walked. The sedan chair was used only
by the very rich.

Shop Early
Freda Beard, 1930

Unlike the Underground posters which rarely showed a bus or Tube train, the LCCT posters often included a brightly lit tramcar, no doubt, to encourage Londoners to choose this means of transport over those of its competitors. Artistic licence was always used to portray a much more spacious interior than passengers would have found, as can be seen in the 1928 and 1929 posters on the previous spread.

Shop Early
C E Montford, 1932

This was the last Christmas poster to be
issued by the LCC Tramways, as by the
summer of 1933 they were absorbed into
the Underground Group.

THE END

With much of London's tramway
network running down the centre of
the street, there was always going
to be a conflict with other forms
of transport. This was as much a
problem for the passenger as it was
for the tramway itself.

Thank You Mr Motorist
J S Anderson, 1932 and 1933

These two posters by Anderson
were issued in the last two years of
the LCC's tramway operations and
show the hazards of travelling by
tram rather than its pleasures. They
were aimed directly at the private
motorist and appealed, hopefully,
to his better nature. Unfortunately
this was a battle that the tramways
in London would not win as shortly
after this they began to be replaced
by trolleybuses and then the
motorbus.

Thank you Mr. MOTORIST

ANDERSON—

1933

Published by LONDON COUNTY COUNCIL TRAMWAYS, 23, BELVEDERE ROAD, LONDON, S.E. 1

BIOGRAPHIES

Leslie S Abbott
1 poster for the LCCT 1927

Frederick Adcock, fl 1909–1933
Adcock painted pictures of London buildings and scenes and illustrated several books about London including one on Highgate. His work can be found on postcards of the period.
1 poster for the LCCT 1933

John Stewart Anderson
Anderson studied at Wolverhampton School of Art and the Royal College of Art. He designed posters for the Underground and Shell in the 1930s.
1 poster for the LCCT 1933

Freda Beard, fl 1920s–1930s
Freda Beard was a portrait painter and commercial artist. In the 1920s and 1930s she designed many posters. Her clients included the Underground, the British Empire Exhibition and the Royal Mail Line. In 1928 she designed the cover for Pall Mall magazine. She exhibited twice at the Royal Academy.
4 posters for the LCCT 1927–1932

Dorothy Helen Bedford, born 1897
Dorothy Bedford studied at the Central School of Arts and Crafts. She was a landscape painter, illustrator, wood engraver and art teacher. She lived in London.
1 poster for the LCCT 1923

Alfred Edmeades Bestall, 1892–1986
Bestall won a scholarship to the Birmingham Central School of Art. In the 1920s he studied at the Central School of Arts and Crafts. He produced paintings for The Amalgamated Press and illustrations for Punch and Tatler and illustrated over 50 books including those by Enid Blyton and Whitcombe's story books. From 1935 to 1965, Bestall wrote and illustrated the Rupert Bear stories in the Daily Express, and continued to produce covers for the Rupert Bear Annual until 1973.
1 poster for the LCCT 1925

René Blair
3 posters for the LCCT 1929–1930

G Stanilaus Brien
G Stanilaus Brien was born in Poland. He was a lino-cut artist and exhibited at the Redfern Gallery in London between 1930 and 1931. It appears that for a while Brien worked with F Sherwin under the name Hobo Bros. Brien designed posters for the Underground, the LNER and Shell. He also illustrated and designed covers for books including Puffin.
2 posters for the LCCT 1927–1929

Pieter Irwin Brown, born 1903
Brown was born in Rotterdam, and studied at the Royal Academy, Amsterdam 1921–1923. He travelled in Europe and Africa working as an artist. In London, he worked for Leigh Breton Studio and set up a design business 'Ralph and Brown Studios' with Rickman Ralph. He designed posters for the LMSR, GWR and the Underground Group. In the 1930s he travelled to Indonesia, Japan and China, where he produced Japanese style woodblock prints and a poster for the Japanese National Railroad. In the 1940s he worked in America under the name Pieter van Oort. He exhibited prints in China and Japan, and at the Los

Angeles County Museum. In 1946 he moved to New York.
25 posters for the LCCT 1925–1933

Oliver Burridge, d. 1954
Burridge studied at Cental School of Arts and Crafts . He was a graphic illustrator and printer. In the 1920s and 30s he designed a number of posters. During World War Two he worked for the Ministry of Information where he met the artist Beric Young and typographers Leon French and William Morgan. In 1945 they founded London Typographical Designers (now LTD Design Consultants). Burridge left the company to manage his family's printing business.
2 posters for the LCCT 1925–1926

G E Butler possibly Butler, George Edmund, 1872–1936
Butler emigrated to New Zealand in 1883 and studied at the Wellington School of Design. In 1892 he joined the Wellington Art Club, becoming a painter of seascapes. In 1898 Butler studied at the Lambeth School of Art, and the Académie Julian in Paris. Back in New Zealand in 1900 Butler exhibited widely and taught art. In 1905, he returned to England and taught art at Clifton College. A noted portrait and landscape artist, Butler was elected to the Royal West of England Academy in 1912. He exhibited at the RA, the Royal Scottish Academy and elsewhere. He was an official war artist.
1 poster for the LCCT 1933

Leslie Carr, fl 1920s–1950s
Leslie Carr was a painter of urban maritime and architectural subjects. He designed posters for the LNER, SR, British Railways and the British Grand Prix in 1950. Other clients included Morris cars, Stewart & Arden and the Motor Magazine, becoming its Art Director in the 1960s. He was a war artist during the second world war.
1 poster for the LCCT 1926

J L Carstairs, fl 1927–1930s
J L Carstairs designed a poster for Peterhead in the 1930s and had a cartoon of Hitler published in Punch in 1934.
1 poster for the LCCT 1927

Tony Castle, 1891–1971
Tony Castle was an artist and illustrator. He designed posters for the LNER, as well as a number of book jackets and other posters.
7 posters for the LCCT 1926–1929

Lance Cattermole, 1898–1992
Lance Cattermole studied at Central School of Arts and Crafts from 1922–23 and at the Slade School of Fine Arts 1923–1926. He designed a poster for Ulster Transport and several for British Railways from the late 1940s to 1960s. Cattermole showed at the RA, ROI, the RBA and widely in the provinces. His work is held by the National Army Museum.
1 poster for the LCCT 1933

Leonard Cusden fl 1933–1950s
Leonard Cusden was a poster designer whose clients included the GWR, LNER and British Rail. During the war he designed propaganda posters. After the war Cusden was the Art Advisor to the Royal Society for the Prevention of Accidents (ROSPA), and with H G Winbolt he produced sixty to seventy posters a year for ROSPA.
1 poster for the LCCT 1933

Verney L Danvers (fl 1920s to 1950s)
Danvers was a graphic designer and poster artist. In the 1920s and

1930s he designed posters for Shell, LNER, Southern Railway and British Railways, as well as for the fashion house Bobby & Co Ltd and Skegness Advancement Association. For some years he ran a school of commercial art and in 1926 he wrote the book 'Training in Commercial Art'.
1 poster for the LCCT 1926

Edmunds
1 poster for the LCCT 1928

Frederick William Charles Farleigh (John Farleigh), 1900–1965
Farleigh was apprenticed in 1914 to the Artists Illustrators Agency and studied art at the Bolt Court School. On leaving the Central School of Arts and Crafts, he taught at Rugby and back at the Central School of Arts and Crafts, where he was appointed head of book production in 1947. He was commissioned by the Postal Congress Union, London Transport, and Poole Potteries amongst others. A noted book illustrator, he was a member of the Society of Wood Engravers. Farleigh exhibited at the RA, the Leicester Galleries and Lefèvre Gallery. In 1940 he was chairman of the Arts and Crafts Exhibition Society.
5 posters for the LCCT 1922–25

G Fitzgerald
1 poster for the LCCT 1929

R F Fordred
4 posters for the LCCT 1932–33

Faith Gaskell
1 poster for the LCCT 1928

Agnes D Gower
1 poster for the LCCT 1925

Frederica Graham
Frederica Graham studied at the Central School of Arts and Crafts in the 1920s. She was a wood engraver and painter.
1 poster for the LCCT 1925

Hammond
Miss Hammond studied at the Central School of Arts and Crafts in the 1920s.
1 poster for the LCCT 1922

W Gale Harris
2 posters for the LCCT 1929–30

Margaret Curtis Haythorne, born 1893
Margaret Haythorne studied at the Liverpool City School of Art c1915. In the 1920s whilst at the Central School of Arts and Crafts, she worked with Muriel Jackson on painted decorations for one of the staircases. Haythorne exhibited in Liverpool and at the RA, the NEAC, and the Redfern Gallery in London with the Society of Wood Engravers, of which she became an associate member in 1924.
2 posters for the LCCT 1922–24

Hobo Bros
This is believed to be G S Brien and F Sherwin.
1 poster for the LCCT 1929

Muriel Blomfield Jackson, born 1901
Muriel Blomfield Jackson was the daughter of the architect A Blomfield Jackson. She studied at the Central School of Arts and Crafts in the early 1920s. Muriel was a wood engraver, portrait painter and muralist. She lived in London and exhibited at a number of venues including the RA, NEAC, Redfern and in America between 1923 and 1940. Her work is held in the Art Institute of Chicago.
2 posters for the LCCT 1922–24

K James
1 poster for the LCCT 1932

I Jephson
Miss Jephson studied at the Central School of Arts and Crafts in the 1920s.
1 poster for the LCCT 1923

F Roberts Johnson fl 1931–1947
F Roberts Johnson designed at least one book for the Vision press in 1947.
1 poster for the LCCT 1931

Morris Kestelman 1905–1998
Kestelman studied at the Central School of Arts and Crafts from 1922–5 and then at the RCA from 1926–9 where he developed an interest in theatre. In the 1940s his theatre designs included works at the Old Vic and Sadlers Wells, In 1946 he designed murals exhibited at the Upper Grosvenor Gallery, Sally Hunter Fine Art and the Boundary Gallery. The V&A, Arts Council and Contemporary Art Society hold his work.
1 poster for the LCCT 1925

Maud Klein
Maud Klein studied at the Central School of Arts and Crafts. She was a wood engraver. She lived in London and exhibited at the RA in 1929.
1 poster for the LCCT 1924

W Langlands
Langlands designed 2 posters for the Underground Group in 1930.
1 poster for the LCCT 1933

Frank Marsden Lea, born 1900
Lea studied at Nottingham Art School from 1916–1917 and then at Manchester School of Art.
He was a portrait painter and commercial artist. As well as posters he illustrated some magazines.
5 posters for the LCCT 1928–1932

Harold McCready, 1930
1 poster for the LCCT

C E Montford
1 poster for the LCCT 1932

M K Mountain
3 posters for the LCCT 1930–1931

A Murray
Murray was represented by the artist's agent R P Gossop, who was also a highly respected commercial artist.
2 posters for the LCCT 1931

G Milton Norris
Norris lived in Notting Hill, London and exhibited at the Royal Institute of Oil Painters in 1928 and 1929.
1 poster for the LCCT 1926

Edward G Patterson
Patterson studied at the Central School of Arts and Crafts in the 1920s.
2 posters for the LCCT 1922–1923

Leslie R Porter
Porter studied at the Central School of Arts and Crafts in the mid 1920s.
5 posters for the LCCT 1925–28

Reginald G Praill fl 1915–1927
Reginald Praill was a highly respected printer at the Avenue Press where he taught lithography to C R W Nevinson and Tom Purvis. He designed posters for the LNER, LMS and LBSCR as well as a poster for an exhibition of war relics and cartoons at Hampstead Town Hall.
1 poster for the LCCT 1927

R & B Studios (Ralph & Brown)
(See Pieter Irwin Brown)

Monica Rawlins, 1903–1990
Monica Rawlins studied at the Central School of Arts and Crafts (1925–1928) under Leon Underwood. She exhibited at a number of venues between 1925 and 1930.
1 poster for the LCCT 1926

J G Rennie
In the 1960s Rennie illustrated programmes of the Opera House in Manchester.
2 posters for the LCCT 1932

Frank P Restall
Restall studied at the Central School of Arts and Crafts. He designed 2 posters for the Underground Group and later worked in the Printing Department of Herriot Watt College. He retired in 1964.
4 posters for the LCCT 1922–23

Herbert Kerr Rooke 1872–1944
Rooke studied at the Royal College of Art and at the Slade School. He also studied or taught at the Central School of Arts and Crafts in the mid 1920s. He lived in London and Sutton in Surrey. Rooke was a marine and poster artist. He designed a poster for the British Indian Steam Navigation Company. He exhibited widely between 1894 and 1927, including several times at the RA.
3 posters for the LCCT 1924.

Rowles
This is probably S C Rowles who designed two posters for the GWR.
1 poster for the LCCT 1928

Sells Ltd
The advertising agency Sells Ltd opened in London in 1869. By 1900, it was the largest agency in the world with offices in London, Edinburgh, Paris and Montreal. The agency was still operating in the 1950s, but no longer exists.
1 poster for the LCCT 1932

R P Sleeman
4 posters for the LCCT 1931

Francis Howard Spear 1902–1979
Spear studied at the Central School of Arts and Crafts. He then studied stained glass at the Royal College of Art, where he also taught in the late 1920s. Spear was also a lithographer and a member of the Senefelder club. His prints are held by Aberystwyth University. His early glass was made at the Glass House. From the 1920s he designed stained glass windows including the east and west windows of Glasgow Cathedral in 1958 and Guildford Cathedral. He lived in Reigate.
3 posters for the LCCT 1923–24

Starr
1 poster for the LCCT 1930

Van Jones fl 1920s–1941
Van Jones was a poster designer. His clients included the LNER in 1941.
2 posters for the LCCT 1927

Edward Henry Seymour Walters 1899–1972
After serving in the Navy, Walters went first to Oxford university and then in 1923 to St John's Wood School of Art before moving to the Central School of Arts and Crafts from 1924–1927, where he studied typography and concentrated on printing. In 1929 he set up a printing business, designing many book illustrations. In 1941 he became master of Marlborough College where he ran the Marlborough College Press. Later he ran the Bromsgrove School Press. In the 1960s he worked with the Carmelite Fathers' St Albert's Press.
1 poster for the LCCT 1926

S M White
Although it is believed that White studied at the Central School of Arts and Crafts in the 1920s a note pinned to the artwork implies that he may also have been a conductor with the LCC Tramways.
1 poster for the LCCT 1922

G M Widmer
It is believed that Widmer studied at the Central School of Arts and Crafts in the 1920s.
1 poster for the LCCT 1923

Lawson Wood 1878–1957
Lawson Wood studied at the Slade School, Heatherley's and at Frank Calderon's School of Animal Painting. From 1896–1902 he was the principal illustrator for C Arthur Pearson Ltd. He left to work freelance. He is well known for his humorous animal subjects and contributed to magazines such as The Graphic, The Strand, Punch, and The Illustrated London News. His own books included Noo–Zoo Tales 1922 and Meddlesome Monkeys, 1946. He had a factory producing toys to his own designs. He exhibited at the RA and elsewhere.
3 posters for the LCCT 1931–1933

Mary I Wright
Mary Wright studied at the Central School of Arts and Crafts in the 1920s.
4 posters for the LCCT 1924–1928